pocket posh

• • • • • • • • •

take care

Inspired Activities
for **Balance**

pocket posh®
· · · · · · · · · ·
take care

Inspired Activities
for **Balance**

Andrews McMeel
PUBLISHING®

We all need some time to focus on ourselves. It's easy to become overwhelmed—by work, by home responsibilities, by the news of the day. It's important to step away, relax, and recenter. *Take Care: Inspired Activities for Balance* invites you to practice small moments of self-care through mindful activities, inspirational words, and thought-provoking journal prompts.
Take some time for yourself.

. . . take care.

"The world nowadays is so complex and fast-paced that knowing how to ground oneself in the present moment is an absolute necessity to make sense of the world and to continue learning, growing, and contributing what is uniquely yours to contribute in this world."

—*Jon Kabat-Zinn*

```
J T W E S T M R K C Z B
N A Z J N R O E P I I E
I B C U S I T T A T N D
E L A K O A H H C N D G
C E V K F H E G I A I X
E A S T A C R U F L A E
A R C T I C K A I T N C
Z X Q U E E N D C A X A
```

find and circle

Four highest playing cards	✓ O O O
Four oceans	O O O O
Four female relatives	O O O O
Four pieces of furniture	O O O O
Two opposing cardinal points	O O

honeybee breathing

This breathing exercise, also called Bhramari Pranayama, engages the power of breath, sound, and vibration to calm your mind.

STEP 1: Find a comfortable place to sit, close your eyes, and try to be aware of your body.

. . . .

STEP 2: With your jaw relaxed and facial muscles loose, breathe in, and then on the exhale, make a low buzzing hum in your throat.

. . . .

STEP 3: Focus on the way the buzzing vibrates throughout your body—not only in your throat, but inside your mouth, in your sinuses, and behind your eyes.

. . . .

STEP 4: Repeat this breath cycle—calming breath in, buzzing exhale—at least six times.

. . . .

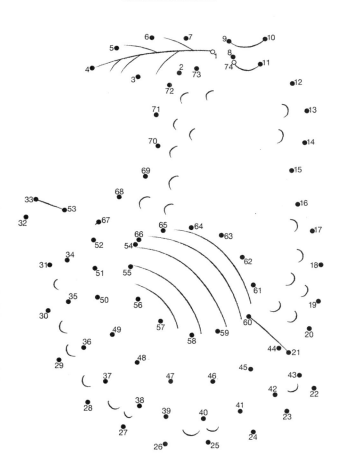

practicing gratitude

Practicing gratitude improves mental resiliency and promotes emotional balance. When we stop focusing on our stresses and worries and take the time to name the good things in our lives, we come away with a more balanced perspective.

What is something in your life that you are grateful for? Your morning cup of coffee? A chat with a friend? Nothing is too small to appreciate.

. . . .

. . . .

. . . .

. . . .

. . . .

. . . .

. . . .

"Our body is an incredible doorway into the present moment. Our mind can be anywhere: past, future, lost, reactive, spaced out, daydreaming, ruminating, angry, anxious . . . but our bodies are always in the present moment. If we can remember to bring our minds into our bodies—just feel a body sensation or two—while we are listening, we have immediate access to the present moment."

—*Diana Winston*

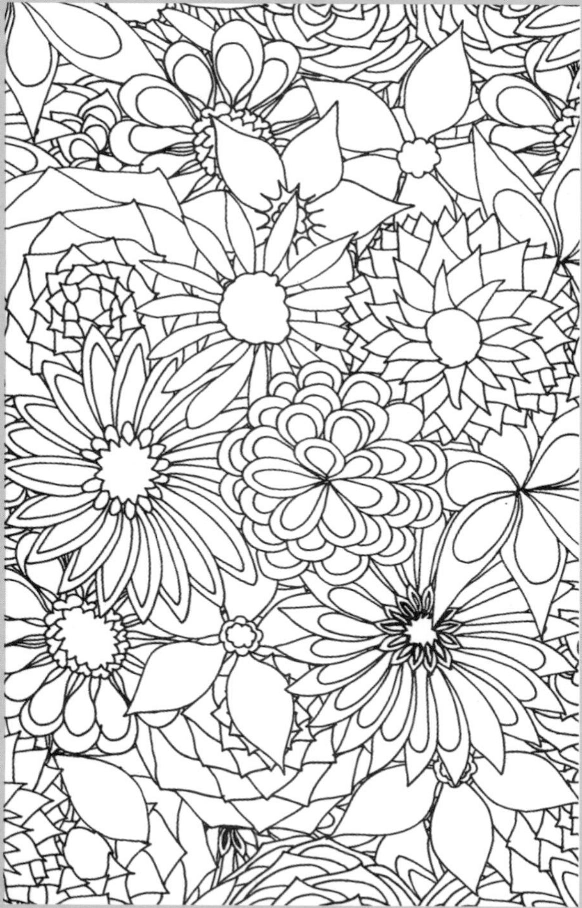

COMFORT By Fred Piscop

ACROSS

1. Comfortable, slip-on shoes, for short
5. Aid in wrongdoing
9. __ pants (comfortable wear)
11. Florida citrus city
12. Birds in a V formation
13. Easy __ (comfortable place to relax)
14. __ cuisine (gourmet fare)
16. Comfortable place to take a nap
19. Cuddle up comfortably
23. Actress Longoria or Mendes
24. To the rear, on a ship
25. Corn serving
26. A scented __ may produce a comfortable atmosphere
28. Flat-topped hill
29. Event with bucking broncos
31. Get comfortable and watch a __ at home
34. Sings like Ella Fitzgerald
38. The Ram, in the zodiac
39. Comfort food that can be made in a Crock-Pot
40. Men and women in blue
41. Rainbow shapes

DOWN

1. Stir-fry flavor enhancer
2. Be in arrears
3. Just-OK grade
4. The younger Obama daughter
5. Feels sore
6. Sheep's call
7. Football great Manning
8. Sailor, slangily
10. Get comfortable with a cup of hot __
11. Eight-piece group
15. In need of a meal
16. Short period of time, for short
17. Eggs, in a biology lab
18. Supporter of a sports team
20. Comfortable shirt
21. __ Vegas
22. The Disco __ (the '70s)
24. Balm-yielding plants
27. Removes moisture from
28. Coffee/chocolate combo
30. Upper-left PC key
31. __ 'n' cheese (classic comfort food)
32. Gold, to the Conquistadors
33. High-ranking person, for short

35. ___ guitar (imaginary instrument)
36. Comfort from an RN, for short
37. Bro's sibling

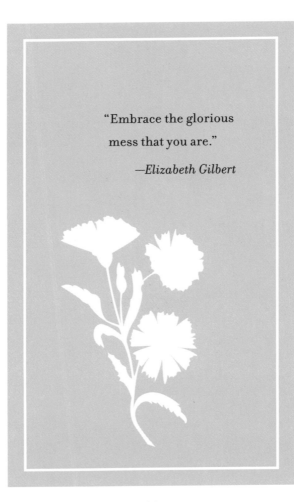

"Embrace the glorious
mess that you are."

—*Elizabeth Gilbert*

J M M A Z A V I R Z R B
J U A A P X U E R E J C
D U L R Y R B G B A V E
O H N Y C M I O U Z N L
U A Z E E H T L X S X P
B I X C K C P E R U T I
L R E V O T E E T H K R
E D S I N G L E L E F T

find and circle

Eight months	⊘○○○○○○○
Three baseball hits	○○○
Two things that are commonly brushed	○○
Two four-letter countries	○○
One way to turn	○

15

sense of peace

The world can be a chaotic place, and it's often hard to slow down. But it's important to balance our responsibilities by taking care of the person tasked with them—ourselves. So try to think about what helps you decompress. What are five things that help bring you a sense of peace? Write them down below and try to take the time to do at least one of them this week.

1. ....

2. ....

3. ....

4. ....

5. ....

"You're likely pursuing your goals because you believe they will make you happy. Remember that when you start letting your goals pull you into a stressful state of mind. If you focus on the good things around you, you'll feel that happiness that you think you need to chase. This will make you much happier in the long term, and, of course, right now."

—*Henri Junttila*

find and circle

Nine motor vehicles	⊘○○○○○○○○
Sherlock Holmes creator (first/middle/last name)	○○○
Three consecutive months	○○○
What "CD" stands for	○○
Vast Russian region	○

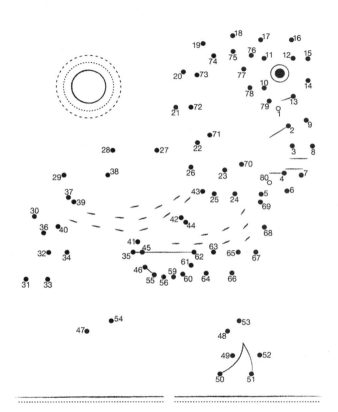

calm waters meditation

Imagine inner peace as a smooth, crystal clear lake.
Visualize the surface of the water. Like a real lake,
intrusive thoughts—to-do lists, anxieties, negative
self-talk—may bubble up and break the calm, but the
surface of the water—our potential for mindfulness
and clarity—eventually returns to stillness. Ripples
may come, but water wants to find its level, wants to
find calm.

"We can choose to be affected
by the world or we can choose
to affect the world."

—*Heidi Will*

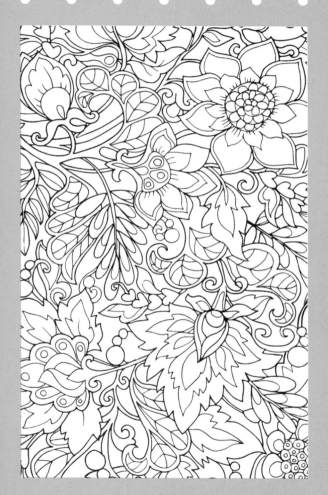

Harmony By Fred Piscop

ACROSS

1. Voice in a four-part harmony
6. Runs on TV
10. "Ebony and __" (song with the words "live together in perfect harmony")
11. Be in harmony
12. Analyze grammatically
13. Union general at Gettysburg
14. "Hold Me" Grammy winner K.T.
16. Man's name that means "harmony"
19. Bring into harmony
23. Collectible cartoon frame
24. Pig's home
25. Took a chair
26. Discipline requiring harmony of yin and yang
28. The Bee __ (Britain's "first family of harmony")
29. Talked ceaselessly
31. Having melody and harmony
34. Early birds' catches
38. Cropped up
39. Letters sent via PC
40. Racetrack figures
41. In recent times

DOWN

1. Helpful hint
2. Longoria of "Desperate Housewives"
3. Neither here __ there
4. "Citizen Kane" director Welles
5. Some deli loaves
6. Athlete's representative
7. Nest-egg investment, for short
8. "Harmony in __" (Matisse painting)
9. Get an eyeful of
11. Peace and harmony
15. Language of old Rome
16. Play a role
17. Grassy expanse
18. "The Greatest" of boxing
20. Take advantage of
21. Scotsman's denial
22. Visitors from other worlds, for short
24. Oil-yielding rock
27. Lacking couth
28. Garden figurine
30. New Harmony founder Robert
31. Living-in-harmony principle
32. O'Hare's airport code

33. Auction assent
35. Totally uncooked
36. $1,000,000, informally
37. Like a fox, it's said

"Your emotions are meant to fluctuate, just like your blood pressure is meant to fluctuate. It's a system that's supposed to move back and forth, between happy and unhappy. That's how the system guides you through the world."

—*Daniel Gilbert*

find and circle

Six four-letter words ending in "X"	⊘○○○○○
Four mountain chains	○○○○
Four highest playing cards	○○○○
Two snakes (five-letter min.)	○○
NYSE: ____ ____ Stock Exchange	○○

take the cake

Sometimes we're so hungry for positive reinforcement that we settle for crumbs of attention and respect when we really deserve a whole meal . . . and dessert. Don't sell yourself short. What makes you feel valued? Write some ideas below. Be open with yourself and others about what you want and need. You're worth it.

· ·

· ·

· ·

· ·

· ·

· ·

· ·

· ·

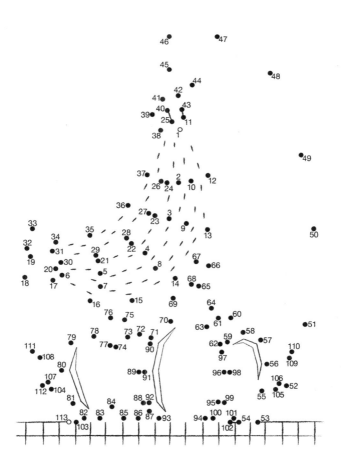

musical meditation

STEP 1: Choose a song to play or any sound recording that appeals to you. It doesn't have to be musical.

STEP 2: Sit in a comfortable chair or on a cushion. Close your eyes. Pay attention to your breathing.

STEP 3: Listen closely to the sounds around you. Focus your attention on the textures and rhythms, the pitch, and the vibrations.

STEP 4: Take a long, deep breath in through your nose, and try to fill your lungs completely. Breathe out through your mouth.

STEP 5: Be aware of how your body responds as you listen. Does your breath begin to follow the beat or repetition of the sound? Does the song or sounds make you feel calmer or more excited?

STEP 6: Spend a minute or two mindfully focusing on these sensations and your breath.

"When walking, walk.
When eating, eat."

—*Zen proverb*

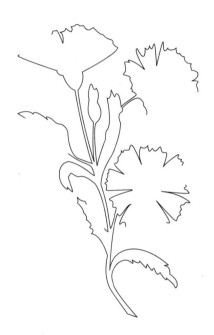

Home By Fred Piscop

ACROSS

1. Home, informally
5. Scatters, as seed
9. Makes sketches
11. Place in the home for a barbecue
12. Raring to to
13. Clearly understood
14. Enjoy a home-cooked meal
16. Comfy home
19. Home, figuratively
23. NPR host Shapiro
24. Tupperware topper
25. Hive occupant
26. Homeowner's place to putter
28. One who may assist in the home
29. Tennis great Chris
31. Feng shui may help you optimize the __ in your home
34. "Humble" home
38. Sax larger than an alto
39. Stately home
40. An au __ may help out with housework
41. Golfers' props

DOWN

1. President before JFK
2. Lyricist Gershwin
3. Comedian's bit
4. "Home __ Home"
5. Relaxing home installation
6. Like non-Rx meds
7. Big name in game consoles
8. The Old __ (home, affectionately)
10. Mrs., south of the border
11. Practiced, as one's trade
15. "To __ own self be true"
16. Broken-down horse
17. The Big Band __ (the '40s)
18. Knight's title
20. Offensive stat in baseball
21. Media mogul Turner
22. Start of a bray
24. Crowbar, essentially
27. An interior designer can spiff up your home's __
28. Facing the pitcher
30. Ewe's mate
31. Longtime NASCAR sponsor
32. Split __ soup
33. Singer DiFranco
35. __-hit wonder
36. Anonymous John
37. Hospital crisis ctrs.

"Don't save things for a special occasion. Every day of your life is a special occasion."

—*Thomas S. Monson*

```
O  N  E  V  A  D  A  R  Y  N  G  D
K  H  D  W  H  I  T  E  S  A  E  E
A  H  I  R  Z  X  N  V  E  G  O  R
K  A  Z  O  I  R  Y  E  M  I  R  S
S  W  X  Y  U  V  Z  R  A  H  G  A
A  A  B  O  N  D  E  S  J  C  I  X
L  I  J  M  A  I  N  E  A  I  A  E
A  I  V  O  Y  A  G  E  Z  M  X  T
```

find and circle

Eight U.S. states	⊘○○○○○○○
Two words that mean "trip"	○○
Two transmission gears	○○
Ian Fleming creation (first/last name)	○○
Colors of the Swiss flag	○○

"If you want to be happy, be."

—*Leo Tolstoy*

balance, literally

Focusing on our physical sensations can be a helpful mindfulness exercise, and the more unique the sensations are, the more our brains pay attention. One way to kickstart your brain's responsiveness is to practice your balance, literally. Try balancing on one foot for twenty seconds. Focus your eyes on different points around you and pay attention to what that does to your bodily sensations.

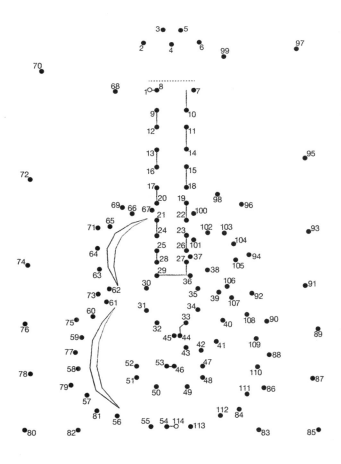

"This is life, and imperfection is beautiful . . . don't be afraid of that."

—*Dylan O'Brien*

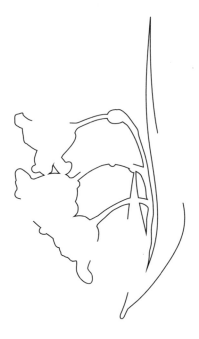

Nature By Fred Piscop

ACROSS

1. Enjoy a nature trail
5. One of Columbus's ships
9. Nature photographer Ansel
11. Dr. Seuss's nature-conscious character
12. The "M" in DMV
13. Really ticked off
14. Minor quarrels
16. Nature's balm
19. Stared wolfishly
23. Sales agent, for short
24. Neither fish __ fowl
25. Bartender's "rocks"
26. __ Nature (the environment, personified)
28. Double-reed instrument
29. Saudi natives
31. Attenborough who narrates the nature series "Planet Earth"
34. Setting of undersea nature shows
38. Furry "Star Wars" critters
39. "Nature" essayist Ralph __ Emerson
40. Restaurant's listing
41. Civil uprising

DOWN

1. Partner of Swiss, in sandwiches
2. Wedding promise
3. Cartoon feline Krazy __
4. Overdo it on stage
5. Like the Vikings
6. Lyricist Gershwin
7. __ Geo (nature channel)
8. Lumberjack's tool
10. __ Lanka
11. Career military person
15. Fauna's partner in nature
16. Biceps locale
17. The Lion, in the zodiac
18. __ out (decline)
20. BBQ morsel
21. Nature-friendly prefix
22. Ruby of "American Gangster"
24. Social goofballs
27. Poetic form inspired by nature
28. Coveted movie award
30. Violinist's need
31. Joe Biden's party: Abbr.
32. Leave speechless
33. Rocket scientist Wernher __ Braun
35. Yalie
36. Needless bother
37. __-for-profit organization

"I hope that in this year to come, you make mistakes. Because if you are making mistakes, then you are making new things, trying new things, learning, living, pushing yourself, changing yourself, changing your world."

—*Neil Gaiman*

```
D C Y H A R E T W O K E
Z E X C N T J U L E S L
W G E I E H N H S V R U
O L X R V R E T O E A M
L Y V C E E V R U R E G
F N Z U L E E O T N B O
J X F S E C S N H E X A
L I O N S E A L W X Z T
```

find and circle

Nine four-letter mammals	✔ O O O O O O O O
Four prime numbers	O O O O
French sci-fi novelist (first/last name)	O O
Two opposing compass directions	O O
Event held under the big top	O

sensory stillness

STEP 1: Gather three to five different small objects from around your home and place them in a bag.

. . . .

STEP 2: Find a comfortable place to sit and take a few deep breaths in through your nose, out through your mouth.

. . . .

STEP 3: Without looking inside your bag, spend some time feeling the objects inside. Note their shape, weight, and texture. Focus on the ways they feel in your hands and how they are different from one another.

. . . .

STEP 4: Continue calmly breathing and practicing mindful awareness of your objects for a few minutes.

. . . .

STEP 5: Before you get up, check in with your body. Wiggle your fingers and toes, and notice your breath. Gradually bring your awareness back to the room around you.

. . . .

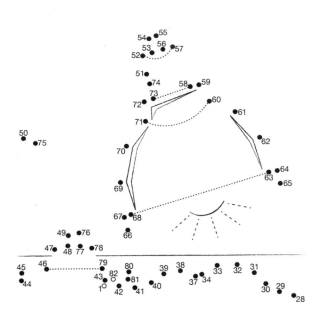

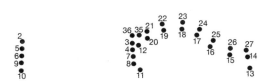

```
M Z D P S J W E Z G X V
B U D E I E O O N Z S T
A O L X E N A I L G G E
R C O E A R K L N F R R
R E G C R C N I E Z A R
I A Z A E O V L K V Y I
E N E H I A O B L U E E
R B C L S M T E A L Z R
```

find and circle

Seven four-letter mammals	☑○○○○○○
Five four-letter colors	○○○○○
Two common types of bank accounts	○○
Two seven-letter words containing three "R"s	○○
Two words formed from A-C-E-N-O	○○

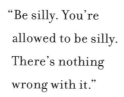

"Be silly. You're allowed to be silly. There's nothing wrong with it."

—*Jimmy Fallon*

peace By Fred Piscop

ACROSS

1. Bird that's a symbol of peace
5. Peace-keeping alliance since 1949
9. Greek goddess of peace
11. Ancient Athenian lawmaker
12. Doesn't have
13. __ branch (peace symbol)
14. Florida citrus city
16. From the beginning
19. John who sang "Give Peace a Chance"
23. Stevens who sang "Peace Train"
24. Pas' mates
25. Ram's mate
26. Hebrew word for "Peace"
28. Metal fastener
29. Pleasant odor
31. Run off to the Justice of the Peace
34. Monk's superior
38. Kidney-related
39. "Peace on __, goodwill towards men"
40. From __ (all-inclusive)
41. Indy 500 or Boston Marathon

DOWN

1. Noisy tumult
2. Unrefined metal
3. Two-finger peace gesture
4. Fund, as a college
5. Ryan who hurled seven nohitters
6. Muhammad who was named a U.N. Messenger of Peace
7. "Mazel __!"
8. White Monopoly bill
10. Upper-left PC key
11. Shoe bottoms
15. Site of Crockett's last stand
16. Room coolers, for short
17. Slangy denial
18. Approximate landing time, briefly
20. Prefix meaning "new"
21. Hooting bird
22. Tennis court divider
24. Tasty mushroom
27. Bolivian city whose name means "the peace"
28. Peace-loving elephant of kidlit
30. West of "I'm No Angel"
31. The Disco __ (the '70s)
32. "__ bygones be bygones"
33. Yoko who joined 19-Across in a "bed-in for peace"

35. Bikini top
36. Like a drug that doesn't
    need an Rx
37. Word often ignored in
    alphabetization

"People are their most beautiful
when they are laughing, crying,
dancing, playing, telling the
truth, and being chased in a
fun way."

—*Amy Poehler*

```
J A D P J G Z F E E T P
E E T O A X L C Y N Z E
S M E L S C I O A K F E
E A M P A T I I V G R L
E T A T C N D F N E E F
H C Y R R N T I I O E E
C H A Z I E R I N C Z E
S P E E C H S U C X E B
```

find and circle

Seven words with "EE" in the middle	⊘○○○○○○
Four oceans	○○○○
Boxing ____	○○○
Spanish one, two, three	○○○
Fifth month	○

65

"Be driven, be focused, but
enjoy every moment because
it only happens once."

—*Alicia Keys*

```
P   P   S   Z   S   H   J   D   V   R   G   S
A   E   J   P   T   U   N   E   E   G   K   Y
R   A   R   A   R   A   M   T   A   C   C   R
A   M   M   U   L   I   N   M   A   N   A   O
G   A   Z   O   K   I   N   L   E   Z   S   T
U   N   P   X   W   V   S   G   X   R   T   S
A   A   S   C   I   E   N   C   E   G   L   I
Y   P   A   U   T   U   M   N   Z   H   E   H
```

find and circle

Four countries starting with "P"	⊘○○○
Four seasons	○○○○
Three school classes	○○○
Two styles of pants	○○
Fortified residence for royalty	○

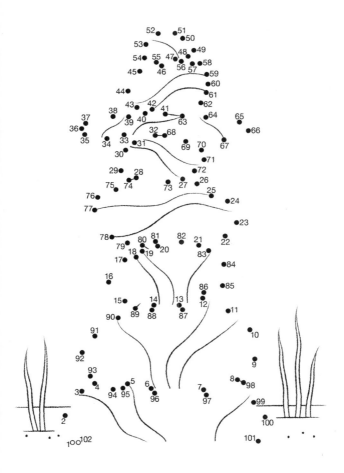

69

find and circle

Five four-letter countries   ✓○○○○

Four joints   ○○○○

Three shirt sizes   ○○○

Two eight-letter words   ○○

Independence Hall ringer: The ____ ____   ○○

natural balance

Shinrin-yoku, or forest bathing, is a Japanese term for mindfully spending time in nature. Time spent away from distractions, out in whatever nature is available to you, has mental and emotional benefits. Whether it's a walk around your block or a meditative hike in the woods, focusing your attention to the sights, sounds, and smells of the outside world can help change your perspective.

"Success isn't about how much money you make; it's about the difference you make in people's lives."

—*Michelle Obama*

S Z X A L B A T R O S S
S W K C L O G N G X C Y
O G A V G T A N Z S A A
C O H N O C I K E B N C
K O Z O I M R L Z A O H
C S B L A O I X V D E T
U E E L T M H O U R K Y
D P F S P E R H E R O N

find and circle

Eight water-loving birds	⦻○○○○○○○
Three four-letter things worn on the foot	○○○
What "mph" stands for	○○○
Two five-letter boats	○○
The opposite of good	○

74

"Instead of trying to make your life perfect, give yourself the freedom to make it an adventure, and go ever upward."

—*Drew Houston*

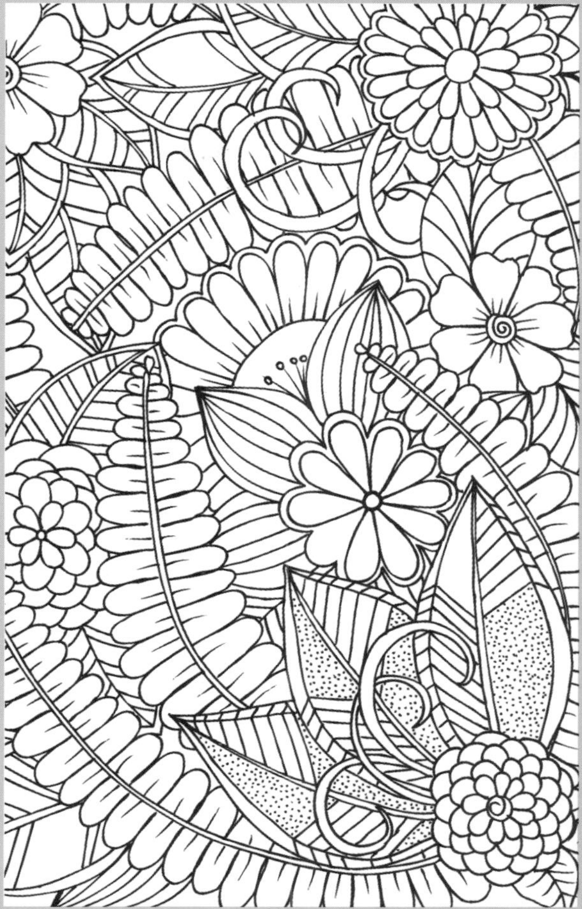

Relaxation By Fred Piscop

ACROSS

1. Place for a relaxing soak
5. See 40-Across
9. __-ski (relaxation in a lodge)
11. Helium-filled airship
12. Postage unit
13. __ as a goose (relaxed)
14. Hank who clubbed 755 homers
16. Mend, as socks
19. Relaxed, like a soldier
23. Period of history
24. Room coolers: Abbr.
25. Female deer
26. Relaxing style of music
28. __, calm, and collected (relaxed)
29. __ swing (place to relax on a veranda)
31. Native of Havana
34. Hourglass or stopwatch
38. Loan shark's overcharge
39. Place to ski
40. With 5-Across, roadside place to relax
41. Take a __ off (relax)

DOWN

1. English majors' degs.
2. Well-put
3. Lead-in to "la la"
4. Macho type
5. __ time (time to relax)
6. __ de Janeiro
7. Letters on an ambulance
8. Gorilla or chimp
10. Relaxing getaway
11. Rorschach test shapes
15. Marathon runner, e.g.
16. Room to relax in
17. "__ we there yet?"
18. Like steak tartare
20. Fuss and bother
21. The Great Lakes' __ Locks
22. Moray or conger
24. Ecstasy's opposite
27. In pieces
28. __ out (relax, slangily)
30. Dollar fractions: Abbr.
31. Mangy mutt
32. Find a purpose for
33. Commuter's conveyance
35. Bovine call
36. Emissions-regulating org.
37. Bullfighter's cape color

"If you're lucky
enough to be
different, don't
ever change."

—*Taylor Swift*

find and circle

Five dairy products	⊘○○○○
Four words ending in "ZZ"	○○○○
Three deli meats	○○○
Three consecutive months	○○○
Twelve-chime times	○○

take a break

It can be difficult to balance our responsibilities
and take care of ourselves. But taking the time to
give yourself a break can make you more productive.
For every few hours of work, take a five-minute
mindfulness break. Do some deep breathing,
practice a short meditation, or take a walk around
the block or even just the room. Giving yourself a
break will reenergize your mind and spirit and leave
you ready to tackle the rest of the day's challenges.

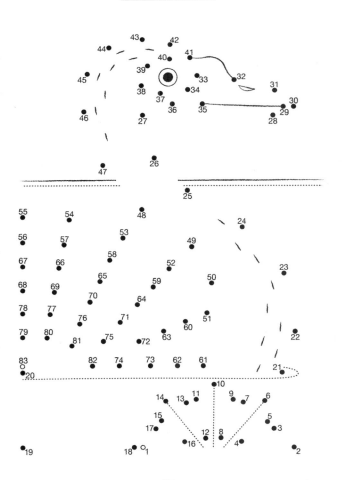

83

"It takes courage to grow up and become who you really are."

—*E. E. Cummings*

conscious community

Social and emotional needs are just as important to our well-being as our physical ones. Who in your life makes you feel valued, whose opinion do you trust, who is someone you feel comfortable sharing yourself with? Write down their names and try to find some time this week to reach out to one or more of them. Tell them what they mean to you, or just say hi. Take some time to maintain the connections that tether us to one another and make us stronger as people.

. . . .

. . . .

. . . .

. . . .

. . . .

. . . .

. . . .

SPRING By Fred Piscop

ACROSS

1. Showy spring bloom
5. Spring school dance
9. Bird that's a harbinger of spring
11. Steamy spot at a spa
12. Part of an act, on stage
13. __-craftsy
14. Italian resort isle
16. Stravinsky's "The __ of Spring"
19. Spring holiday
23. Period of history
24. Comic Rickles
25. "Spring is in the __!"
26. Popular spring break destination in Mexico
28. Boats like Noah's
29. Birthday cake's horizontal section
31. Do a spring chore
34. Purplish spring bloom
38. Analyze grammatically
39. Big name in cameras
40. "To Spring" and "To Autumn," for two
41. Gardener's springtime buy

DOWN

1. Tax-collecting org.
2. Huge bird of myth
3. "May __ excused?"
4. "__ you asked . . ."
5. "I love __ in the springtime . . ." (Porter lyrics)
6. Furrow in a dirt road
7. Carry-__ (some airline luggage)
8. __ Queen (spring festival figure)
10. Museum-funding org.
11. Clear kitchen wrap
15. Showy spring bloom
16. __ room (place to play)
17. Nest-egg investment, for short
18. Beachgoer's skin tone
20. Road repair stuff
21. Apt. feature, in ads
22. $200 Monopoly properties: Abbr.
24. Guitarist Allman
27. Student group
28. Astrological sign of spring
30. 90-degree bend
31. USN noncom
32. Young fellow
33. Poet's "before"
35. Tell an untruth
36. Card in a royal flush
37. Ill-bred fellow

"You get to define the
terms of your life."

—Cheryl Strayed

```
C M A C H Z C H A D C A
X U B I O L O G Y C Y I
E C B X M O U N T R P D
L A J A Z F U J I O R O
I N S T E P H E N A U B
H A H A W K I N G T S M
C D Z C O L O M B I A A
C A M E R O O N Z A X C
```

find and circle

Nine countries starting with "C"	✓○○○○○○○○
English theoretical physicist (first/last name)	○○
Japanese volcano: ___ ___	○○
Science of living matter	○
Speed-of-sound ratio: ___ number	○

93

"Many people worry so much about managing their careers, but rarely spend half that much energy managing their lives. I want to make my life, not just my job, the best it can be. The rest will work itself out."

—Reese Witherspoon

```
J Y H E A R S E L I M O
M E V A N H Y E Y X Z S
J A E X Z K L C L A J I
I B Y P C Y S A U R C B
X U Z U O I X R J T O E
A S R D D J U N E H N R
T T C O M P A C T U A I
A M B U L A N C E R N A
```

find and circle

Nine motor vehicles	☑○○○○○○○○
Sherlock Holmes creator (first/middle/last name)	○○○
Three consecutive months	○○○
What "CD" stands for	○○
Vast Russian region	○

"It's the choice that you have to wake up every day and say, 'There's no reason today can't be the best day of my life.'"

—*Blake Lively*

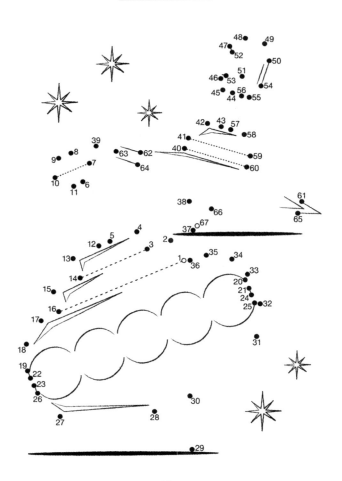

name your feelings

A key component of emotional balance is
understanding our emotions in the first place.
Being conscious of our feelings and naming them
helps us better know ourselves. Take some time to
think about different feelings—start with sadness,
joy, longing, pride—in different ways.

If this feeling were a person, what would they be like?
If this feeling were a color, what would it be?
If this feeling were a place, what would it feel like?
If this feeling were music, what would it sound like?

"Never, ever underestimate the importance of having fun."

—*Randy Pausch*

Water By Fred Piscop

ACROSS

1. Enjoys a buffet
5. Low __ is the best time for beachcombing
9. Beachcomber's find
11. Take a transatlantic vacation on this ship
12. Rent this craft at a lakeside resort
13. Choose from a menu
14. Zuppa di __ (trattoria fish dish)
16. Place to ride a beach buggy
19. Build a sand __ on the beach
23. Prefix meaning "equal"
24. Website ID
25. Place to go sailing, perhaps
26. Place to moor a pleasure boat
28. A surfer may "catch" one
29. Track meet official
31. Car parker at a restaurant
34. Place to rent for a shore vacation
38. Seafood that may be baked on the beach
39. Get the better of
40. You may "catch" these at the beach
41. Thor and Zeus, for two

DOWN

1. Upper-left PC key
2. Cry of discovery
3. Commandments count
4. Place to ski
5. You can ride a bike with balloon __ on the beach
6. Politically unaffiliated: Abbr.
7. Barely-passing grade
8. Make a blunder
10. Robert E. of the Confederacy
11. All-stops subway train
15. "Beat it!"
16. Like a low-watt light bulb
17. Uncle Sam's land
18. Neither fish __ fowl
20. "Unknown," on a sked
21. Washroom, for short
22. Hurricane center
24. Meter and liter, for two
27. List components
28. Incorrect
30. __-friendly ("green")
31. Pre-TiVo device
32. Pie __ mode
33. Produce eggs
35. Prefix meaning "recent"
36. Defective firecracker
37. Photo __ (media events)

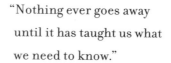

"Nothing ever goes away
until it has taught us what
we need to know."

—*Pema Chödrön*

"Silence can be scary, and we often feel a need to 'fill the space' with conversation, music, or noise, but silence can be healthy for your mind, and can promote mindfulness and relaxation. Try switching off the radio on your drive to work. You might find that you enjoy the time alone with your thoughts."

—*Janet Miller*

notes

· ·

· ·

· ·

· ·

· ·

· ·

· ·

· ·

· ·

· ·

· ·

· ·

notes

solutions

SOLUTIONS

JACK, QUEEN, KING,
ACE—ATLANTIC,
PACIFIC, INDIAN,
ARCTIC—DAUGHTER,
MOTHER, NIECE, AUNT—
CHAIR, TABLE, SOFA,
BED—EAST, WEST

3   word roundup

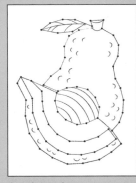

5   dot to dot

10   spot the differences

12   crossword

SOLUTIONS

DECEMBER, OCTOBER,
AUGUST, MARCH,
APRIL, JUNE, JULY, MAY—
SINGLE, DOUBLE, TRIPLE—
TEETH, HAIR—IRAN,
PERU—LEFT

15   word roundup

AMBULANCE, HEARSE,
TRUCK, LIMO, JEEP,
TAXI, BUS, CAR, VAN—
ARTHUR, CONAN,
DOYLE—MAY, JUNE,
JULY—COMPACT, DISC—
SIBERIA

18   word roundup

19   dot to dot

24   spot the differences

SOLUTIONS

26 crossword

APEX, LYNX, JINX,
HOAX, ONYX, IBEX—
HIMALAYAS, ROCKIES,
ANDES, ALPS—QUEEN,
KING, JACK, ACE—
PYTHON, COBRA—
NEW, YORK

29 word roundup

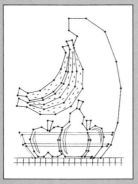

31 dot to dot

36 spot the differences

D	I	G	S				S	O	W	S
D	R	A	W	S		P	A	T	I	O
E	A	G	E	R		L	U	C	I	D
			E	A	T	I	N			
N	E	S	T		H	E	A	R	T	H
A	R	I		L	I	D		B	E	E
G	A	R	D	E	N		A	I	D	E
			E	V	E	R	T			
S	P	A	C	E		A	B	O	D	E
T	E	N	O	R		M	A	N	O	R
P	A	I	R				T	E	E	S

38 crossword

MICHIGAN, GEORGIA,
NEVADA, HAWAII,
ALASKA, MAINE, TEXAS,
OHIO—JOURNEY,
VOYAGE—REVERSE,
DRIVE—JAMES, BOND—
WHITE, RED

41 word roundup

44 dot to dot

48 spot the differences

50 crossword

BEAR, GOAT, MULE,
SEAL, WOLF, DEER,
HARE, LION, LYNX—
TWO, THREE, SEVEN,
ELEVEN—JULES, VERNE—
NORTH, SOUTH—
CIRCUS

53 word roundup

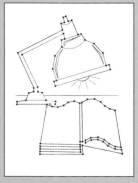

55 dot to dot

MULE, DEER, SEAL, BEAR,
LION, MOLE, WOLF—
PINK, GOLD, TEAL, BLUE,
GRAY—CHECKING,
SAVINGS—TERRIER,
BARRIER—CANOE,
OCEAN

57 word roundup

60 spot the differences

62 crossword

FREEZE, CHEESE,
SPEECH, FEET, BEEF,
JEEP, PEEL—ATLANTIC,
PACIFIC, INDIAN,
ARCTIC—MATCH,
GLOVE, RING—UNO,
DOS, TRES—MAY

65 word roundup

PARAGUAY, PANAMA,
POLAND, PERU—SPRING,
SUMMER, AUTUMN,
WINTER—SCIENCE,
HISTORY, MATH—
SLACKS, JEANS—
CASTLE

67 word roundup

69 dot to dot

CHAD, PERU, CUBA, IRAN, IRAQ—KNUCKLE, WRIST, ANKLE, KNEE— SMALL, MEDIUM, LARGE—ASTEROID, ASTERISK—LIBERTY, BELL

70 word roundup

ALBATROSS, FLAMINGO, PELICAN, STORK, HERON, GOOSE, DUCK, SWAN— BOOT, CLOG, SOCK— MILES, PER, HOUR— YACHT, CANOE—BAD

74 word roundup

76 spot the differences

B	A	T	H				A	R	E	A
A	P	R	E	S		B	L	I	M	P
S	T	A	M	P		L	O	O	S	E
			A	A	R	O	N			
D	A	R	N		A	T	E	A	S	E
E	R	A		A	C	S		D	O	E
N	E	W	A	G	E		C	O	O	L
			P	O	R	C	H			
C	U	B	A	N		T	I	M	E	R
U	S	U	R	Y		S	L	O	P	E
R	E	S	T				L	O	A	D

78 crossword

YOGURT, BUTTER, CHEESE, CREAM, MILK—FRIZZ, JAZZ, FUZZ, BUZZ—TURKEY, SALAMI, HAM—APRIL, MAY, JUNE—MIDNIGHT, NOON

81 word roundup

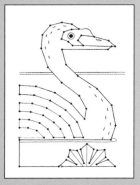

83 dot to dot

88 spot the differences

121

I	R	I	S			P	R	O	M
R	O	B	I	N		S	A	U	N	A
S	C	E	N	E		A	R	T	S	Y
		C	A	P	R	I			
R	I	T	E		E	A	S	T	E	R
E	R	A		D	O	N		A	I	R
C	A	N	C	U	N		A	R	K	S
		L	A	Y	E	R			
C	L	E	A	N		L	I	L	A	C
P	A	R	S	E		L	E	I	C	A
O	D	E	S			S	E	E	D	

90 crossword

CAMEROON, CAMBODIA, COLOMBIA, CROATIA, CANADA, CYPRUS, CHILE, CUBA, CHAD—STEPHEN, HAWKING—MOUNT, FUJI—BIOLOGY—MACH

93 word roundup

AMBULANCE, HEARSE, TRUCK, LIMO, JEEP, TAXI, BUS, CAR, VAN— ARTHUR, CONAN, DOYLE—MAY, JUNE, JULY—COMPACT, DISC—SIBERIA

95 word roundup

97 dot to dot

102 spot the differences

104 crossword

E	A	T	S					T	I	D	E
S	H	E	L	L			L	I	N	E	R
C	A	N	O	E			O	R	D	E	R
			P	E	S	C	E				
D	U	N	E		C	A	S	T	L	E	
I	S	O		U	R	L		B	A	Y	
M	A	R	I	N	A		W	A	V	E	
			T	I	M	E	R				
V	A	L	E	T			C	O	N	D	O
C	L	A	M	S			O	N	E	U	P
R	A	Y	S				G	O	D	S	

108 spot the differences

Andrews McMeel Publishing
a division of Andrews McMeel Universal
1130 Walnut Street, Kansas City, Missouri 64106

www.andrewsmcmeel.com

20 21 22 23 24 RLP 10 9 8 7 6 5 4 3 2 1

ISBN: 978-1-5248-6696-9

Editor: Allison Adler
Art Director: Julie Barnes
Production Editor: Jasmine Lim
Production Manager: Tamara Haus

ATTENTION: SCHOOLS AND BUSINESSES
Andrews McMeel books are available at quantity
discounts with bulk purchase for educational,
business, or sales promotional use. For information,
please e-mail the Andrews McMeel Publishing
Special Sales Department: specialsales@amuniversal.com.